GIVE YOUR EMPLOYEES

C.R.A.P.

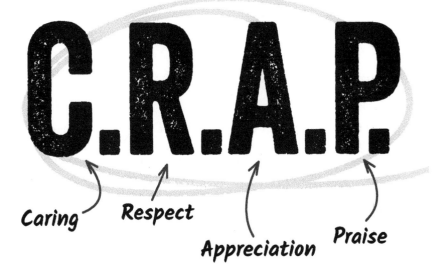

Caring   Respect   Appreciation   Praise

AND 7 OTHER SECRETS TO EMPLOYEE RETENTION

JEFF KORTES

ISBN: 978-0-988307-018

Book design by AbandonedWest Creative, Inc.

INTRODUCTION:
PUT YOURSELF IN A POSITION TO WIN

THERE ISN'T AN organization anywhere that doesn't have a problem *of some type* with turnover. If you think that's not true, you are probably losing a ton of money. Your turnover may be relatively low, but is it still costing you money, hurting customer satisfaction, lowering quality, or perhaps resulting in the loss of that occasional top performer who really impacts your organization. If you work the tips in each section of the book, and begin taking action on other ideas you think of as you read, you will get results. The ideas in this book have worked for me, and I have seen them work in other organizations.

I'm not a believer in setting some target number. Why? Because then the number becomes the goal and you will start to make excuses if you don't hit the number, or worse yet, start manipulating your data to justify not hitting your number. I have seen people hang on to a lousy employee because they are paranoid that someone will get on them about their employee retention number. In some cases, as you will see later, you will see it is to your benefit to get rid of a lousy employee. What I do advocate, is that you begin working the activities, develop a strategy after a short period of time and execute on that strategy. The results will follow, I guarantee it!

As you start trying the activities listed in every chapter, you will see your retention strategy begin to develop. Performing the activities is like building a block tower just like the ones we all built as kids. We built it one block at a time and no two towers ever looked alike. How sturdy the tower is depends on you. The shape of the tower is up to you as well. When I present my "Give Your Employees C.R.A.P.®" speech, I tell the participants that their goal is to develop their own tower. Make the tower your own.

How hard you work at your retention tower, or who else in your organization you get involved, will be up to you. The first step is that you got the book. The second is that you have started to read it. If once you start to read you begin to try the tips I offer, you are on your way to developing a successful retention strategy for the department, division, company or entity you are responsible for. At the risk of sounding self-serving, you will know if you are serious if you go to the boss and tell him, "We need one of these books for all our supervisors and managers!" Why? Because then you have started to put your money where your mouth is. Once you start to ante up some cash, you will want to see the fruits of your labor and the momentum of multiple leaders in the organization working the process together.

As you start to work the chapter tips, or other ideas you see, you will see a strategy start to emerge. You will also start to see some success—which will get you hungry for more. I don't advocate that you read everything and then

Art by Nick Aringer

try to develop some grand plan. Just slowly start trying the tips. That's the beginning of building your retention tower. What you are doing is not different than what famous athletes do. Tiger Woods talks about "putting himself in a position to win on the back nine on Sunday." He knows that a tournament is 72 holes. His goal is built over the course of the previous 63 holes, shot by shot. Your retention tower is built block by block. Systematically!

ABOUT THE AUTHOR

JEFF KORTES has more than 30 years of experience in the human resources field. During that time, he has worked in heavy manufacturing, construction, textiles and software development businesses. He has spent his entire career having to attract, retain and energize employees at all levels of the organization, while working for companies such as Midas International, SPX, ConAgra, Regal Ware, Inc., Wigwam Mills and The Quaker Oats Company. He has helped clients as small as 10 employees to be able to compete against large employers as they seek to attract and retain the talent needed to survive and thrive as a business. Jeff has experienced the pressure of having to retain people in booming economies and has fought the "retention wars" while looking for intellectual talent in software development, skilled trades in manufacturing plants and on construction sites, as well as, production people in a hosiery mill. He has always taken a "no nonsense" approach to human resources that is based on common sense and the use of sound, fundamental approaches to dealing with employee retention. His decision to write this book was driven by his disappointment that no one had written a book that applied these fundamentals in an easy to understand and apply approach. He observed that organizations get too fancy and lose sight of the fundamentals which, if done well, can produce incredible employee retention results in even the most competitive marketplace. That philosophy is at the heart of this book.Jeff knew that the tactics he had used in the past work. He then researched and spoke with other Human Resources professionals and line managers to get their thoughts on what has worked for them. One common theme came out over and over in his work, research and discussions that was at the heart of effective employee retention: **C.R.A.P. Caring, Respect, Appreciation and Praise.** Those organizations and managers that gave their employees C.R.A.P. had excellent employee retention. When combined with 7 other key fundamentals, you will have a "no nonsense" approach to your employee retention. He is a member of the National Speakers Association (NSA) and is a frequent speaker to companies and associations on the topic of employee retention. Jeff runs his own company helping organizations to recruit, energize, develop and retain their best people.

TURNOVER:
WHAT'S IT COSTING
YOU?

I HAVE SEEN countless formulas and studies to determine the cost of turnover in an organization. Everything I have seen indicates that the best measure is roughly three months of salary for every person who leaves. I have also seen a formula that the cost of turnover for entry-level employees is 30-50% of annual salary, 150% of annual salary for mid-level employees and as high as 400% of salary for high-level employees. Some people might say these numbers are overstated, but think about the cost of a middle-level manager who walks out the door and a key deadline is missed because no one can fill their shoes or a major opportunity is not capitalized on.

A third formula I have seen, calculates that the cost of turnover is 25% of the annual salary. Those numbers can be staggering if you are running at 10% turnover. Imagine the bottom line impact if you could cut turnover in half, to 5%. The savings are huge even when looking at lower-level employees. I used to see this when software developers would leave an organization I was with. We could calculate how much a delayed product roll-out would cost us—the numbers were mind boggling. This is particularly the case when talking about knowledge-based businesses. All your resources walk on two feet and when that person walks out the door on you, so does their knowledge.

Regardless of what number you pick as a formula to calculate the cost of turnover, stick with it. Don't start adjusting your measures so you start to feel good about where you are going. If you do that, you will not feel good as you see profits start to deteriorate. When that happens, you will see your good people start to jump ship because they realize you aren't addressing the problem and that you are in denial. *Once turnover starts to accelerate, it is very hard to slow it down much less put a stop to it.*

I recommend that you classify your turnover as good, bad or neutral. Some turnover is good. Yes, that's what I said! There are times when you have to fire people or permanently reduce your workforce. That's reality. If you want to take that into account when calculating your turnover by all means do so. Just don't play games with the numbers to make yourself feel good about your lousy turnover. Whatever measurement you chose, use the same measurement over time. When you fire a non-performer it should be good turnover. When a top performer leaves to go elsewhere, it is bad turnover. Neutral turnover can be things such as an employee who left the organization to retire. Classify your turnover and start tracking it in the three categories. This also forces the managers to discuss with HR whether the turnover was good, bad, or neutral. That dialog enables management to see if you have a manager who is realistic or making excuses because they are not doing what they need to do to retain people. Trends will become very evident in various operating units, plants or departments. If you are a Plant Manager, General Manager, VP or owner, you want to be monitoring your turnover numbers and asking questions about what activities are taking place to reduce it!

Perhaps, most importantly, your ability to retain talent is going to be a matter of survival. It is that simple. With any amount of solid economic growth, we will demographically not have the people that are needed to staff our factories, wait our tables, write our software or perform almost any job we have to fill. There are simply too many people leaving the labor market and too few entering. We have been on this collision course for years but the recession that started in 2008 and the anemic recovery that has followed, has lulled organizations to sleep, thinking people were in abundance. Only now are leaders of these organizations beginning to see that talent is becoming scarce. It is going to get a lot worse. Part of the answer to having enough people to run your organization, much less grow it, is the ability to retain the people you do hire.

From this point forward you need to adopt a "no excuses" mentality when it comes to bad turnover. You will look at your bad turnover and realize it is turnover that is not acceptable—and then start to take action to address it. *No excuses!*

NO NONSENSE **NOTES**

- Everyone's approach to retention is different. Decide what your strategy will be.

- Determine how you will calculate the cost of turnover, then stick with the calculation you pick to measure future performance.

- Not all turnover is bad! Turnover can be classified as good, bad, or neutral.

- Adopt a "no excuses" mentality about accepting bad turnover.

AS A MANAGER, give your employees C.R.A.P.® The more C.R.A.P. you give them the better off you are. Caring. Respect. Appreciation. Praise. I learned early in my career that C.R.A.P. was the most important secret to drive employee retention. C.R.A.P. works and as you begin applying C.R.A.P. and the other 7 secrets to employee retention, you will see your employee retention improve.

Caring

I do believe that most managers truly care about people. I believe you can care and still get the job done. Unfortunately, with the frenzy of work, we forget that is an integral part of being a good manager or supervisor. It is particularly important if you're in human resources. The pace of work combined with unpleasant incidents dealing with people, tends to jade managers over time. Hopefully, reading this section will jolt you out of that state of mind as you are reminded of the importance of caring. If you don't care for people, get out of management. It's as pure and simple as that. If you don't, you will be miserable for your entire career.

Caring is at the heart of being a *great* supervisor, human resources person or executive. People know if you do, and they know if you don't. People have this innate instinct and can tell. It's something you just can't fake. Assuming you care, the key is knowing how to show your people that you care. People are far less likely to quit if they know you care about them. It no longer becomes a decision that is simply business; it becomes personal. More often than not, people quit because of a boss. They are far less likely to quit a caring boss.

Part of caring is knowing your people. This is crucial to being a caring boss. Where did they go to college? What do they like about their job and what do they hate? How many of you don't know the names of your employee's children or what activities they are in? What does their spouse or significant other do for a living? What do they like to do on the weekend? Are their parents even alive? You need to know these things because that is what motivates them to work and impacts how they are able to perform at work.

Showing you care is harder for a boss to handle than anything else. Our concern for privacy has made us reluctant to get to know people. Big mistake. Although organizations do not forbid supervisors from getting to know their people, they send out the subliminal message to them that doing so somehow crosses this line of privacy. The best managers ignore this subliminal message and get to know their people. Not in a prying and intrusive way, but in a way that enables them to understand what's important to their people. Those important things are what motivate people to come into work day in and day out and get the job done for you.

People like to talk about what goes on in their lives, what frustrates them, what gets them excited and all kinds of other things. **Listen to them.** The insight they will provide into who they are is invaluable as you work with them in the future. That insight can be applied when looking at what projects to place them on or why their productivity has been slipping in the last month. **Most important of all, it makes them feel good that you listened because your listening tells them you care enough about them to take the time.**

> Make it a point to learn one new thing every day about your people. In a year, imagine the insight you will have that will make you a better manager or supervisor.

As a caring boss, you must have a willingness to protect your people. Repeatedly you hear me refer to employees as "your people." They are yours to protect. They are the corporate equivalent of your flock and you are the shepherd. Your job is to keep them safe from the corporate wolves, while at the same time making sure they do what they are expected to do.

Your people will come under attack from other managers, or often time from your own boss. Your job is to make sure they don't get "thrown under the bus." When something goes wrong, organizations look for someone to blame. People will make mistakes. Would a shepherd leave one of his sheep behind when the wolf was after it? If you didn't answer with a resounding "no," then you need to take a good hard look at yourself as a leader. Remember, ultimately, you are responsible for your people and what they do. You can't delegate responsibility for events that happen in your department. People know that and watch to see how you act. Accept that responsibility and take the heat, instead of immediately looking to have someone else take the blame so you don't look bad. Your people respect that and respect you for it.

That respect will pay off big time when you need that extra time on a project or special touch they bring to a customer issue. As a professional recruiter, I begin to salivate when I call in trying to recruit someone and they have just been thrown to the wolves by their boss in a meeting. They have just seen how little they matter to their boss. The organizations and managers I recruit for don't do that, and I will tell a prospective candidate just that. That is a huge selling point for most candidates. Why? Because too many bosses throw their people to the wolves.

Remember, 75% of the people feel the worst thing about their job is their boss. If you are a lousy shepherd, you are in that 75% and your people will leave for greener pastures. If you become one of the unique group of the other 25%, imagine the competitive advantage you will have when you are trying to retain people!

Like it or not, we hire the husband, the kids, the dog and even the ex when we hire a person. What affects them, affects how your people perform on the job. Ask anyone who has a kid that is in trouble!

Remember, 20% of employees are experiencing some sort of issue in their life at any one time. Those issues have a real impact on the state of mind of your people when they are writing that software program, or not writing it because they are thinking about their daughter who is talking about moving in with that loser boyfriend of hers. Your ability as an organization to quickly connect people with the resources they need to get through the bumps in the road is critical in keeping your people fully engaged and productive. Helping people to do so also sends a very positive message that you truly do care. People remember when you are there for them even if they might never admit it. If you help them thru the tough times, you, begin to seem "human" in their eyes. It is a lot harder to walk out on a person than it is a nebulous entity like a "corporation." I am emphatic about also having an EAP (Employee Assistance Program) that works well. That means it goes beyond just being some "800" number that people call into and get passed on to some provider that they don't really know. EAP should be sending employees to resources that EAP knows will get the job done for your people. An organization's EAP should be performance oriented. After getting someone's name, rank and serial number, one of the first questions they should ask is, "How is this affecting your work?" Makes sense right? After all, that's why you have them there. Here is a quick checklist to test if your EAP is on the right track.

1. Are the number of people who are accessing EAP realistic considering the size of your organization? (Low numbers mean your workforce has less issues than other organizations right? NOT! If they are low, find out why!)

2. Does EAP understand your environment and the problems your people face at work?

3. Have the people answering the phone seen your workplace?

4. Have they been briefed about your organization, culture, etc.

5. Does your EAP provide people with mechanisms to cope at work? (People are going to have issues, but they still have to function at work).

Again, a great EAP sends the message you care about your employees as people at a time when we have depersonalized the workplace and people are viewed as a cog in the wheel of most organizations. If you have an "800" number, strict quality assurance measures need to be in place to ensure it provides top quality care. That initial contact can make or break whether or not an employee quickly gets the right help and is able to get back on track. It's good for business when your people are focused and productive. It's great for your retention. Always remember one of my key rules of retention: people talk! You want them talking about how you helped them, their kids, their spouse, hey, maybe even their dog!

Respect

Everyone deserves respect. They may do something that causes them to lose your respect, but until they do, basic respect is something everyone deserves.

The main way that most managers disrespect their people is that they hire good people and then micromanage them. Micromanaging sends the message you do not trust them or their ability to get the job done. If that is the case, then you have to address that instead of micromanaging them. Micromanaging people is the surest way to drive them from an organization. People hate being micromanaged and it is one of the major reasons that people quit their jobs.

Listening to your people is another one of the best signs of respect. It sends the message that they and their ideas are important and that you are willing to spend time with them. Time is one of our most valued resources and your people know it, so when you are willing to spend the time to listen, you send a message of respect.

Respect is one area that a leader of an area has total

control over. Your boss may be a jerk or you may work in an organization that doesn't value people at the level it should. That doesn't mean that you have to be like that. It certainly makes it tougher if the organization is not in synch with you but it's not an obstacle that can't be dealt with.

Respect is so basic to any relationship among people that I shouldn't even have to write a section on the topic. Unfortunately, respect in the workplace has changed significantly in the past 30 years. Ironically, we talk about it more but give less of it to people. Basic respect is about the simple courtesies of everyday life. Respect is about character and class. Look at the people *you* respect. In 99% of the cases you see that person as having character and being a class act. You may not like them but you will, albeit grudgingly, respect them.

Who's often the worst offender on this topic? In my opinion it's the VP's, Presidents, General Managers and Owners. I hate to say it, but it's as if power and authority causes people to feel like they have the right to act however they please. Maybe that's why many people in these positions are viewed as arbitrary jerks. (I am being kind. If you are a senior level executive or owner reading this, your people will use less kindly terms to describe you in the hallway.) Here is a simple *test* of whether or not your people respect you. If you are pretty sure that the first thing your people talk about is **you** when they get home at night, you have a problem! People will vent immediately to their spouse, significant other or the person they are sitting with in the bar about a lousy boss. If it's you they are talking about first thing, you are probably not viewed very highly!

Your job as a leader is to set the tone in your "sphere of influence," **and this is the area where you should start** first. The simplest ways to set the tone and show respect are to not bark out orders, avoid sarcasm, say "Hello," say "Good morning," and always make time for your people when they need to talk to you. Respectful behaviors are woven into every section of the book because they are that important in employee retention.

Another area that I feel is crucial to demonstrating your respect for people is to never jump to conclusions. If an issue comes up, it is essential that you ask questions, listen to people's sides of the story, and *investigate*. Failing to do so sends the negative message to everyone in your organization that people's opinions simply do not matter. You already know the answer. You have just made the presumption that you know more than they do or that you don't have the courtesy to get their side of the story because you are the boss. Result: You have just started to set a tone of disrespect. That's in addition to getting sued or hauled in front of the Equal Employment Opportunity Commission (EEOC) with a discrimination complaint because you didn't investigate before you acted, and reached the wrong conclusion!

Don't get me wrong. I am not saying don't discipline or fire people if they deserve it. Just make sure they deserve to be fired. There have been countless times in my career in Human Resources that I have fired people and they have admitted they deserved it. They didn't like it but, regardless, I treated them with respect, so the firing was far more positive. And guess what, the other people in the organization respected me because of the way I handled it. I always treated people with dignity and respect.

As an organization, ask yourself this question: How do you treat people when they resign to take another job? This sends a powerful message to everyone else in the organization about whether or not you respect people. I hear from candidates all the time people become lepers upon resigning, or, worse yet, are treated horribly. Your people are watching your every move and absorbing how you treat the people who are departing. Treating the departing person shabbily is often the deciding factor for other people if they are wondering if they want to continue to work in your organization. As a professional recruiter, I get very nervous when people are treated really well during their notice period. Why? Because they often start to feel sad about leaving people they have a good relationship with. That makes them vulnerable to a counter offer or, more easily enticed back in the future if the new organization does not live up to their expectations. People are counseled all the time to never "burn your bridges" when leaving an organization. Organizations should never burn their bridges either by treating a departing person shabbily.

Appreciation

Showing appreciation is another matter. Often we take people for granted. We think that people should know that we appreciate what they do. When you are trying to retain people, why would you leave that to chance? *Show* people you appreciate them! *Tell* them you appreciate them! This is basic motivational theory, yet we fail to take advantage of the opportunity to use a free retention tool. In these days of tight budgets, anything you can do for free, you need to be doing.

There are hundreds of gestures to show you appreciate people. Pick ones that fit your style and incorporate them into your retention arsenal. But, before I leave the issue of showing appreciation, I want to touch on the most important way to show appreciation after the use of praise: food!

Personally, I am a big believer in food! Food seems to be the one thing everyone appreciates and gets people mingling and breaks down barriers. "Breaking bread" is a great way to show appreciation and create some camaraderie in your department, plant or company. Coming from Wisconsin, I found that bratwurst transcends all levels and people appreciate the fact that you took the time to show your appreciation. When I worked in the South it was barbeque. Hey, when in Rome do what the Romans do. Whatever you serve, food is one of the best ways to show your appreciation to your people for accomplishments, a job well done or for simply being a part of your team. Eating breaks down barriers and people talk like at home at the dinner table. When they talk, you listen, get to know them and build some trust. And remember: trust drives retention!

I have seen studies that indicate that as many as 50% of the workforce do not feel appreciated. That is half the people out there that are working. This is a problem that is easy to solve. The easiest way to solve this problem is to tell people when they do a good job. I am not talking about gushing platitudes at people. I am talking about saying to someone when they do things right things like, "Looks good," "Nicely done," and "Keep up the good work." This is a simple acknowledgement that they did something right. People need to hear that; it is important to them.

Often when conducting training, I hear a manager question the need to give appreciation like I just mentioned for "everything" someone does. I am not talking about every time. What I am talking about is on a regular basis. The old school philosophy of your people only hearing from you when they do something wrong is exactly that-old school. If you want get the most out of people, you need to show them appreciation for doing a good job and clearly, 50% of the workforce does not feel that is happening.

"Please" and "thank you," should be the *easiest* of all as

a starting point. Use the words, and use them a lot. They go a long way in taking the edge off of requests we make of our people. People know you want or need something done, yet we often act as if by using the words "please" and "thank you" we are somehow not communicating the urgency of the request. Much of it has to do with the fact that work has gotten faster paced. We are more uptight and have simply become rude because of it. If you build a department or organization where you regularly use "please" and "thank you," you lay the foundation to take respect to the next level.

In his book, "The Fred Factor," Mark Sanborn provides some of the best examples of the behavior that rises from a culture where "please" and "thank you" are evident. If you are a supervisor, applying the principles of the Fred Factor sends the positive message that you not only appreciate your people but respect them as well. The best thing about it is, it feels good! Once it starts, people will pick up on it and you are on your way to building a positive feeling in your area of influence. I don't know about you, but I like to feel good, so why not try it, today. After reading this section commit to saying "please" and "thank you" and begin immediately, *please.*

> Start consciously saying "please" and "thank you" tomorrow, and keep tally to see how many times you do this because it will become habit-forming!

Praise

When someone's actions exceed expectations, they need to be praised. Praise is appreciation on steroids. When a person is praised, it is a big deal. They have exceeded expectations and they need to hear about it in a way that reinforces how their actions impacted the department, the organization and, ultimately, the customer. If you want them to exceed expectations more often, you need to reinforce their behavior with praise. People love it.

Praise is something every manager should want to give out. Praise has four wonderful attributes. **1. It's fast to give.** I can give the type of praise I mentioned in under 15 seconds. **2. It's fun to give.** I don't know about other leaders, but I feel good when I have the opportunity to praise someone. **3. It's free.** Giving praise to one of your people does not cost a dime, which makes it a great tool to drive positive behaviors. **4. Lastly, praise motivates people.** People love praise and want more of it and will, therefore, act in a way to get more of it.

NO NONSENSE **NOTES**

- If you don't care about people, get out of a leadership role!
- Protect your people like a shepherd protects their flock.
- When you hire a person, you hire all of their baggage as well.
- Use an exceptional Employee Assistance Program (EAP), it's worth its weight in gold.
- People talk. Have them say good things about you!
- Treat everyone with respect—always!
- Set a tone of respect in your "sphere of influence."
- Exercise common courtesy. Start with saying "please" and "thank you."
- Investigate prior to taking disciplinary action.
- Treat those who are leaving with respect.
- Praise is free. Use it to show your appreciation and to motivate.
- Break bread with your people. It transcends all levels in the organization and it's better than eating a bologna sandwich for lunch!

SECRET #2:
HIRE THE RIGHT PEOPLE

FACE IT, HIRING is often done when someone quits and the organization is under the gun to replace a person quickly because organizations no longer carry excess people. With no fat to pick up the slack, managers rush to get a "body" to fill a hole. Managers do not evaluate what they truly need in the role and therefore do not capitalize on a golden opportunity to pick the best candidate.

Would you buy a $90,000 piece of equipment without thoroughly deciding on specifications and what you needed that piece of equipment to do? No way! I remember arguing for hours in a staff meeting about the features we wanted on the new coffee maker! If you hire someone and pay them $30,000 per year and expect them to stay with the organization for only 3 years, you have just decided to invest $90,000 in a human asset. I don't know about you, but when I purchase something for $90,000, I do my homework, know what I need and how I am going to evaluate if it is the right piece of equipment. Hiring people should be no different!

There is a simple way to make sure you get the right people—use a systematic approach that uses the following elements.

- **Know what you need.**
- **Train the people who are involved in the selection process.**
- **Hire for "fit," not just for skills.**
- **Don't over hire.**

Know what you need

If you determine what you "must have" and what you "want to have" you will know it when you see it. The belief that you have to look at some predetermined number of people is ludicrous. This isn't a shopping trip to the mall where you are looking for "a pair of pants" and have only a slight idea of what you want. You should KNOW before you start that you want gray pants, the waist size, length, fabric etc. This is crucial so you recognize the right candidate when they walk in the door. If the right candidate comes in, and you decide to look at three more because this is the first one, chances are that person will be gone by the time you get done finding, scheduling and interviewing the other three people it happens all the time. Why? Good people will be snatched up by companies that are decisive and know a great candidate when they see them. As important as the retention component is, also remember that while your job sits vacant, things are not getting done that are costing you money!

Train the people who are involved in the selection process

Sadly, most people you interview are better prepared and more knowledgeable than the people conducting the interview. Answer these questions honestly: Have you ever gone through any formal interviewing training? Has anyone taught you how to prepare for an interview? How to listen to the responses of candidates? I ask these questions all the time when I conduct my "Give Your Employees C.R.A.P.®" presentation. Generally, I get only 20% of the people answering they have received formal interview training. Yet every candidate in the world is reading articles on the job boards, practicing and learning how to respond appropriately to questions. Practice does make perfect and most candidates are pretty good.

Although people can learn to interview by learning on the job, it certainly isn't optimal without some baseline training to get you on the right path. Then, start to monitor your newly trained interviewers. Observe and correct their performance. Once they feel comfortable you will see the difference in how they conduct an interview. For that matter, if you are in HR, get out there and get some formal training yourself!

Hire for "fit," not just for skills

Last and most importantly, you need to be looking for "fit." Studies show that fit is the most important determiner of success on the job. Not whether or not they can do Excel, SAP, or have a Masters degree. "Fit", or chemistry, is what you are after. Chemistry is not if they know key software. Fit are those *traits* that are crucial to a person's ability to mesh with their boss, co-workers and the culture of the organization. Unfortunately, interviewing is one of the least reliable ways to determine fit, even if your interviewers are trained and conduct proper interviews.

I encourage all of my clients to use some form of psychometric testing instrument to help determine fit, whether it is for various traits of personality, ability to learn or mental horsepower. The instruments have become incredibly accurate as they have evolved through the years. They "strip away the veneer" so that an organization gets a look at the real person, and, combined with solid interviewing can enhance your ability to determine fit. By using the instrument, you have just eliminated one more uncertainty that can lead to a poor hire and, ultimately, turnover.

A good friend of mine who specializes in providing these instruments to organizations, uses a Branick device (that's the thing you put your foot in at the shoe store to measure foot size) to illustrate how important fit is to the success of a new hire. You can get a size 8 foot in a size 7 shoe for a period of time, but after a while your feet start to hurt because they do not fit! Just like a person. Most candidates, like politicians, put their best foot forward to get the job, then after about six to nine months, they can't be someone they aren't and their real personality comes out. If you are lucky, your organization is a size 7 and so is the candidate. If not, you and the new person you hired may rub each other the wrong way. Sometimes the fit is close and all is well, but if not, you have just built turnover into your hiring process.

Another advantage of using a psychometric testing instrument is that it gives you incredible insight into how the new person "ticks." The result: you have now reduced the time it takes for the boss and the new person to get to know each other and eliminated one element that can slow the ramp-up time for that person to be productive. If you are *really* intent on ensuring the right fit, have the boss take the instrument as well and let the boss and new person share their results with each other. Do it during the hiring process! What this does is help each party to understand why they act the way they do and helps the boss know how to best manage the new person. The psychometric testing instrument is your "owner's manual." Would you buy a $90,000 piece of equipment and let the equipment supplier drop it off without an owner's manual? No way!

There is another huge benefit of both parties knowing what makes each other tick. Remember, 75% of the people in this country say the worst thing about their job is their boss, right? If the candidate knows what they are getting going into the relationship, they may see they are a bad fit and not take the job either. Again, unnecessary turnover is reduced. If you think I'm nuts, ask yourself how the guy who runs eHarmony.com has made millions of dollars. He uses a psychometric testing instrument to measure compatibility, i.e. fit, to find a good match. When I realized that was no different than looking for the right fit in a new hire, I started using these instruments as an HR guy. I now advocate to the clients I conduct professional search assignments for, to do so as well. Why? They work!

Don't over hire

You are not looking for God in a 3-piece suit! It's great to get a candidate who has everything you want and then some. The problem is, why would this person want your job? And if they do take the job, how long will they stay? Often we see this great candidate who brings more to the table than we actually need. Mom used to say "If it's too good to be true, it probably is." Occasionally that magnificent candidate will come along and it works out well, but not usually.

Over hiring leads to many of the retention issues we have talked about unrealistic desire to grow, fairness, pay etc. When they are all mixed together you are faced with a no-win retention issue. You will expend extensive time and energy dealing with an issue you could have avoided by hiring a person who meets the needs that you have. If it seems too good to be true, it probably is!

TIP

Schedule some interviewer training in the next two months. Get someone who knows how to interview to conduct the training if you are not that person. Result: The people who have to conduct the interviews will be more confident and competent.

TIP

Go online and look at some of the psychometric testing instruments that are available and try some of the demos to see if you can find one that is right for your organization.

Diversity of thought

For years we have heard about how the generations all have a different thought process on how they view work, and life for that matter. People lament that the new generation does not want to work as hard but instead works to live and not lives to work. I actually started to write a section on the generations and was convinced by my wife and youngest son not to. Why? Because it is our experiences that impact us, not the generation we are from. For example, the myth that "old people" (like me) are not technologically savvy is ridiculous. I have seen people my age that are better technologically than people in their 20s. The myth that someone in their 50s wants to coast to retirement. Also ridiculous! It's not the age, it's the fire in the belly. I work harder than 90% of the population because I have that fire even though I am over 50.

Forget about age/generations, race, sex, their accent, sexual orientation, etc. What people think is the key. No one can read minds, so ask your people what they think, what they value, how important work life balance is and where do they see their career going. Assumptions, based on some trait, are what get us in trouble when building our retention tower. Flexibility in your approach is what is needed because the one thing that is true in today's workforce is that we are more diverse. Our different thoughts about work, family, etc. are what drives us. Whether or not we stay with an organization, how many hours we want to work in a week, if we value certain benefits, etc. Your understanding of those thoughts is the starting point in building your retention tower.

Listen to your people and be flexible that's how you will be able to effectively deal with a diverse workforce. Is it easy? No. However, it's easier than you think if you talk to your people, listen to them and act based on the information you hear from them.

NO NONSENSE **NOTES**

- Know what you must have and what you want to have in a candidate and be realistic.

- Fit is **the** most important determiner of success on the job, hire for fit, not just for skills.

- Train anyone that participates in the interview process on how to conduct an appropriate interview.

- Use psychometric testing instruments to improve your ability to determine if you have a proper "fit."

- Ask your people what's important to them, because you can't read minds!

- Flexibility is a must when determining which retention tools are important to a diverse workforce.

SECRET #3:
THE LEADERSHIP DIFFERENCE

ACCORDING TO 75 % of people, the worst thing about their job is their boss. That is a stinging indictment of management today. I have always contended that most people do not retire because they want to. They retire because they get tired of all the nonsense they have to go through at work. Most of that is usually a result of how their boss treats them. If you read nothing more than this section, retention in your organization will improve because your supervisory and management team is the engine that drives retention. The most important person in retaining your best people is their boss. I don't see the term "boss" as a negative as long as the "boss" treats people well and leads in a way that brings out the best in their people. You can have a great boss or you can have a lousy boss. The terminology is not important, the actions are!

The boss is built into every section of the book because the boss and his actions are everything in retention. A company that has great leadership will have great retention, and happy, satisfied, and energized employees. And, let's face it, the vast majority of bosses are not Directors, VPs and Presidents. They are supervisors, team leaders, department managers, plant managers etc. The power and success of an organization is driven by these people more than anyone, even if the VPs and Presidents think it's them. Marcus Buckingham found this to be the case in the studies he conducted in his book "First Break all the Rules." High performing organizations were a function of the managers, not the senior executives. (Buckingham, 1999)

If you are supervising people **at any level**, you need to take a good close look in the mirror at yourself. If you're senior management, you need to take a look at the leaders in your organization as well as yourself. Leaders need to have the skills and value systems required to sustain an organization into the next generation because to 90% of your people, the supervisor is the company! These are the horses you will ride to the finish line. How well you do as an organization depends on the quality of this group.

First, look at their value system. If they are the type of leaders that do not treat people with respect, do not care about their people, make excuses when things go wrong, throw people under the bus, say one thing and do another, carp about things they are asked to do, have turnover in their department or other signs that they are not solid leaders, it's time to act. "First Break All the Rules" is a great read if you want to see the characteristics you should be looking for.

You probably can't do much about someone that has a lousy value system. If they have a lousy value system, get rid of them. This is not an excuse for you to wipe out supervisors who don't always agree with you. It is a call to action to address those supervisors who will never have a value system that sees people as adding value. In most cases, you can train their brains out and nothing will change. Figure out if that is the case and take action. Move them into a non-leadership role or remove them from the organization. Then, replace them with people who know how to lead. Retention will increase immediately in that area. > *Carol!*

Unfortunately, identifying and removing poor managers is not that easy. There is a need to look at how they manage their people. Supervisors that do not delegate, can't make decisions, micro-manage and fail to hold their people accountable will bury your organizations. In many cases, they have fallen into ruts and need to be reminded of their role. In other cases, and this is where it gets tricky, they simply do not have the skills to lead the way their value system would like. The answer: give them the skills. Basic leadership training is one of the most overlooked areas in organizations. Don't believe me? Look at how training budgets are the first thing cut when things get tough. Did I just describe your organization?

The number of large organizations that do not provide uniform, basic leadership skills training on an ongoing basis is mind boggling. The key is uniform, basic, and consistent training over time. If your leadership training does not meet those three criteria, you are missing the boat and losing money because of it. Uniform, basic, and consistent training over time can be used to reinforce the organizations value system and develop skills.

My clients tend to be privately run businesses or stand-alone units that are growing. Why? They are usually led by someone who has a vested interest in the success of the business and they know their supervisors are the key to their success. So, they invest the money because they know they will get a payback. They are not worried about a few bucks spent on training. Maybe that's why they are growing and profitable!

If you are a manager reading this and the organization has chosen not to implement a leadership training series, what can you do? Ask Human Resources. If they give you some excuse why it is not happening, find training on your own and ask if they will pay for it. If they say no, pay for it

> **TIP**
> Find out the last time you or your organization did basic leadership skills training (if ever). If it has been more than three years, schedule a refresher course for everyone. If the training has never occurred call me, or someone like me, to get you that training. Sending your supervisors and managers out to work with your people without any fresh basic skills is like sending an army to fight a war with outdated weapons. The result: You are going to lose the war!

> **TIP**
> Take 30 minutes, sit down in a quiet room, and develop a list with the names of your two worst supervisors or managers. Then, ask yourself if they have the "values" you need as an organization. If not, then develop a plan to change that or remove them from the organization. This may not be the total answer to your supervisory problem but it is a huge step in the right direction!

yourself and go on your own! Invest in yourself. It's your career, not the company's and when your job is eliminated, the facility closes or something else happens, you are prepared. If you are lucky and that never happens, use those skills to be more successful than your peers who sit back and coast.

I'm not trying to clean up the world, only my little corner
Hawkeye Pierce, M*A*S*H

I heard this said over 25 years ago. It has stuck in my mind and influenced my work philosophy. Let's talk about how it should impact your actions as a leader. If you bought this book you are looking for a better way to lead that improves retention. Leadership really comes down to you, regardless of what your organization chooses to do. You can lead in your own department or area. I like the term *sphere of influence* to describe where you can make an impact. I have seen corporations that were employee-relation nightmares, but I worked in one of the plants that was a shining example of how to do everything right when it came to leadership. Why? Because the Plant Manager chose to lead that way and all of his people followed his lead. He led in his own style which was very employee relations oriented despite the overall actions of the parent company.

The same is true whether it's your team or department. Like Hawkeye Pierce, you need to concentrate on cleaning up your area of responsibility. You will drive yourself crazy if you try to solve all of the location or facilities problems, much less the rest of the organization. Concentrate on your sphere of influence regardless of size and create your own little island within the organization by controlling what you can control, which is a lot. What can you control? You can control the following items for sure:

- **Your attitude.**
- **How well you communicate.**
- **How you treat people.**
- **Being a positive example as a leader.**
- **Caring for your people.**
- **Being genuine.**

How you treat your people has more of an impact on turnover than anything else. You have seen it yourself in organizations you have worked in. Certain managers tend to churn through people, even the ones the managers hire themselves. And no one is happy in their departments. They are running the corporate version of a jail. People are doing time because they have to and will get out as soon as they can. Others tend to be people magnets who everyone wants to work for. They have people who will go the extra mile for you and you can feel the positive energy when in those areas.

Look at the lousy ones. Here is what you see them do:

- **They micro manage their people and will not delegate.**
- **They send mixed messages about what they want.**
- **They blame their people for lack of performance or complain that they can't trust the people in their department to get the job done.**
- **Nothing is ever good enough for them.**
- **Take credit for their people's successes.**

The end result? You see a revolving door of people in their department. When asked why their turnover is so high, you will hear excuses like, "I demand more from my people, than other managers," or "You just can't find good people" or "People have no work ethic." It goes on and on. You know who those managers are in your organization. This type of manager will not survive into the next decade because retention will be the biggest challenge facing organizations. Their behavior will not be tolerated because organizational survival will be dependent on keeping turnover low due to a shortage of people to fill jobs.

Your goal: don't be one of them! If you started to get uncomfortable reading those excuses, you need to do a gut check and ask if you are one of those managers. If you are, change or get out of management because you are a major cause of turnover in your organization.

> Conduct a personal gut check right now! Look at the items above and check off if they are you or not. Then look at what you checked and start working on changing yourself. Start today after looking at your list. Be honest with yourself.

Do it for yourself. Stop complaining and lead. It's as simple as that. Your people will love you. You will be happier. Try the tips as you read the book. You will be much happier in your role because you will see the difference, and so will your people.

In the end, how you are viewed is a function of your credibility and whether or not people trust you. If you have those two things going for you, you are going to be a retention magnet. All of the actions and traits discussed in this section and in the book build your credibility and trust. If you have credibility people will trust you. If they trust you, they are far less likely to quit. It's that simple.

Don't complain the next time something doesn't go right. Instead, substitute these words when you talk to your people. "We will find a way to solve that problem." Then watch how differently your people react. You have gone from being a drain on the attitude of the organization to leading by example. Your people will feel better about you and you will feel a lot better about yourself.

I have developed a list of traits that countless employees I have spoken with wanted in their boss. I took that list and had some of the best leaders I know look at the list and add to it. In the end, I came up with a list of 34 traits that the best bosses possess. I call it my "C.R.A.P.py Boss" Questions. In this case, you want someone to say you are a "C.R.A.P.py Boss." You can download the checklist for your use at www.jeffkortes.com. It is a great tool to see where you stand as a leader.

Leaders...Lighten Up and Have Some Fun!

Why do we act like having fun on the job is illegal? It's no wonder that employees struggle to get up in the morning and come in to work. We have moved to "business casual" attire and at the same time have gotten more and more uptight about how we act compared to 25 years ago. Ironically, people in companies now look unhappier than ever.

It never used to be that way. We wonder why people are miserable and always wondering if there isn't a better place to work. I call it the "Grass is Always Greener Syndrome."

More intense competition and fear of getting close to our people has made most organizations humorless. That was particularly the case in the last recession we experienced. If you don't look serious, intense and austere, the notion is that you can't be working very hard. That has become the philosophy in many organizations. What does it need to be? In my opinion, if you aren't enjoying your work you probably are not attacking your work with an energy that customers can feel. You are not very engaged. You are simply putting in your time. The last thing you want is to have employees who feel like they are "doing time." You're not running a jail, you're running a company.

If, by some stroke of luck you develop an environment where people laugh and have fun, the edge you will have on your competitors will be beyond imagination. Why? When your turnover drops, you won't lose knowledge that drives quality and productivity. As an HR person, imagine not having to continuously hire people, or when you do have to, people have heard about your great environment and you have the pick of the best people. That's good enough for me to give it a try.

Think of the difference it would make if your people were looking forward to coming in every morning because they enjoyed their work. Imagine what it would be like if people had fun. Just imagine the following benefits.

- **Lower absenteeism because they want to be there.**
- **More communication among people because they want to talk to each other.**

- An excited, enthusiastic employee speaking with your customers because they want to talk to the customer. The customer can feel it!
- Espirit de Corps within your work group because they do not want to let their work group down.

The benefits are enormous of having people enjoy their job. Part of the enjoyment is to have some fun, or at least to work in an environment that is not uptight. You will always have people who fight you on every little initiative. You know who they are. They're the ones who are never happy, complain about everything, are generally miserable and don't look like they ever have any fun. What can you do to get the ball rolling and start to lighten up and have some fun?

Rule #1: Smile. It goes a long way towards making you feel better and sets an expectation that this is the norm for your people. Guess what, people will start to smile back. I used to joke with people who would never smile by telling them they looked like their dog died. Then I'd jokingly tell them, "C'mon, smile." Guess what, they smiled. Smiling works.

Rule #2: Say, "Good Morning," even if it kills you! A few people will not respond. Ah ha! You have now found your future project. Seek that person out every morning and say "Good Morning" no matter what. Kill them with kindness.

If you are a plant manager, general manager, vice president, owner, president or senior member of leadership, Rules #1 and #2 are essential. People will love you and respect you! Why? Because they are used to top management being a bunch of suits, stuffed shirts and lacking in humor. Smiling and saying good morning does not diminish your professionalism, it enhances it. It makes you a non-jerk. The number of senior leadership people I have seen walk by people in the hall without so much as a nod of the head, smile, or simple acknowledgement is countless. I can't print the adjectives people used to describe them. The result: no one respected them and no one would certainly go the extra mile for them. Bottom line is, it was bad for the business!

Rule #3: Laugh. There is always something to laugh about. Find the humor in situations and laugh about them with your people. Before you know it, you will be laughing with your people and fellow managers and situations that appeared negative will take on a different light.

Rule #4: Don't take yourself so seriously. Seriously! (That's supposed to be an attempt at humor-bad, but at least an attempt.) Life is too short to view everything as life and death. We need to be serious about serving the customer, not serious for the purpose of being serious.

After you start to apply these four basic rules, you can start to look at injecting some fun into your "sphere of influence." But at a minimum, start to follow the four rules. That is the meat and potatoes. Anything beyond that is pure gravy.

If you want to look at having some of the gravy, buy the book Fish Tales. I love the book. You may not do some of the wild and crazy activities they talk about, but you might lighten up a bit and do some fun activities. If you can increase retention in a call center, you can increase retention anywhere (Lundin, 2002).

I am not one of these wild and crazy guys who does karaoke or likes to dress up in weird outfits. That's not me. (Although I have been known to wear a Hawaiian shirt!) I only wish I could be one of those people. The plus side is that I guarantee you have those type of people hiding somewhere in your environment. Let them start to be that person who is inside of them, as long as the customer is taken care of, the parts get out the door, and your quality is what it needs to be. Your job is to create an atmosphere where people feel they can be themselves. Fun will follow. Better yet, tap into their ideas and start to try some of the fun things they think about.

TIP Think about a time at work where you had one of those embarrassing situations or when disaster occurred. Now go talk to one of your co-workers who was there with you. I guarantee you will start laughing! The worst situations seem to be hilarious when we look back on them.

TIP Make it a point to say "Good Morning" and smile when you greet every person in your department, **every** morning! Start tomorrow and keep a log to keep you on track.

TIP Buy the *Fish Tales* book. Read it. Now try to come up with your own type fun at work. Start to develop your "fun" style then ask some of your fun people for their ideas.

NO NONSENSE **NOTES**

- 75% of the people in this country feel the worst thing about their job is their boss. Resolve to be in the other 25% that people talk positively about.
- Provide uniform, basic leadership training on an ongoing basis for your management team.
- Invest in your own training if the company won't invest in you.
- Take ownership of your "sphere of influence" and resolve to make things better in that sphere.
- Control what you can control—that is quite a bit!
- ★ Stop complaining, blaming others, or whining—instead, start to lead.
- Don't take yourself so seriously.
- Laugh.
- See the positives in every situation.
- Smile!
- Say "Good Morning" with a smile.
- Humor is not illegal in the workplace.
- Fun people are hidden in your organization. Find them and tap into their expertise.

SECRET #4: **IT'S NOT ABOUT THE MONEY, NOT TOTALLY**

MONEY IS AN excuse. Managers and companies like to use it as an excuse when they are losing good people. It's a way to rationalize away all the things that they should be doing to retain people but are too inflexible, lack creativity or do not care about their people. This is reinforced by employees who, when they resign, will rarely tell the company the truth because they don't want to burn bridges for the future. The line you always hear, "I got a better opportunity for more money." When questioned they are evasive about their reasons or you receive a "vanilla" exit interview form that tells you nothing.

Realistically, how many people are going to take a job for less money? Not too many people I know. If they do, it's because you don't offer something in your environment. People leave for some other reason and get more money in the process. As a professional recruiter, it is very difficult to entice an employee away from their current job because they are underpaid. If it was all about the money, people would accept a counter offer of more money from their current company every time. It only happens in about 5% of the cases with the candidates that I recruit.

Pay

Don't get me wrong, pay is important. Most of us are not independently wealthy and don't work because of altruism. As you notice, this book was not free! Studies that have been conducted since the beginning of time all come to the same conclusion. In most cases, money will fall anywhere between three and six as the reason for leaving. That being said, money is important. People work to pay the rent, cover the car payment, send the kids to college and to do other things that add to their quality of life.

This is especially true with the millennial generation. They have been raised by mom and dad at a standard of living that is unprecedented in any workforce. Money is something they are used to having and are more driven by it than most generations. They like their toys, technology and their mocha latte grande expresso every day that costs $5 a pop. They are also *more* driven by other factors *you* can control.

The other group where pay is a more important factor is for those people making less than $42,000 per year. People who fall below that bracket tend to be twice as likely to leave than those above $42,000 per year. Makes sense to me. Most people are trying to attain a standard of living that provides a reasonable level of comfort to pay for the things most of us want in life.

As much as possible, your goal is to reduce the impact of pay as a factor in the retention equation. Studies have shown that compensating people near the average, or *slightly* above the average will minimize pay as an issue in employee retention. If you aren't paying competitively, you better be doing everything else right. If you are paying competitively, you have just taken a major step to minimize the impact of compensation in the retention equation. When I used to propose this strategy, I used to immediately hear that it is a competitive market and that we have to watch costs closely. The key is to know what the market is paying for certain skills, then pay at the appropriate level. Communicate that to your people. This is particularly important today because people will go on the internet and pull up statistics of their own from places like salary.com. Beat them to the punch and have *accurate* studies available. Show them the information and discuss it. That will help you to refute *their study* when they say they are underpaid.

I especially want to point out one thing. Notice, I call it compensation, money, or pay. That's how most people view it. My experience with employees is that if you want to irritate them, call it rewards! If you use that term, change it. People don't come to work to be rewarded, they come to get paid. I point this out because it speaks to how we communicate with employees. Most people hate buzz words and see them as a ploy to distract them from the real issue of what you are going to pay them!

How you divide the compensation pie within the organization is crucial. This is as important as how much you pay. Nothing will drive an employee out of the organization faster than paying some slug the same (or close to the same) as a solid or great performer. Don't kid yourself. People have a pretty good idea what the person in the next cube is making and they compare how they perform compared to that person.

If you are a manager reading this, **how you divide** the compensation pie is the one area that most of you have a measure of control over. In most cases you have a say in how you divide the pay pie at the end of the year, at least within certain parameters. Bottom line: <u>Take the money from the lousy performers and give it to your solid and great performers.</u> Unfortunately, most managers split the pie "equally" or pretty close to equally thinking this will keep everyone happy. Sadly, according to *WorldatWork* (December 2001), at most companies there's only about a 10% difference in what we pay our best performers versus what we pay our average performers. Those top performers tend to outperform the average performers by 50%.

If you have <u>great</u> employees, you need to go to bat for <u>them. Ask for more for them and be ready with a sound</u> rationale *why it's good for business and the impact to the business if they leave.* The most that you can be told is "no." Then you know you have to use other tools to help retain that solid performer.

<u>You shouldn't care if your slugs are happy or not. If they don't like it, let them leave, you will be better off.</u> Your good people can always find another job. They're good and other companies will recognize it. As an HR Director, I rarely had a manager come in and say they wanted to take from the poor performers and give it to the best people. If they did, they never got an argument from me. <u>You should not be looking for equality; you should be looking for fairness.</u> Fair *is* paying the top performers more than lousy performers. After all, they are worth more to the organization. When that slug complains, take advantage of the opportunity to start a constructive dialogue about their performance. Tell them they got what they got because of their lousy performance then tell them what needs to change if they want to see more money in the future. Discussions with lousy performers are not fun. Welcome to management. Don't weenie out! I would rather have that

discussion than have to scramble to replace a top performer. **That** is not fun.

I also advocate overpaying people that the business
can't afford to lose. Yes—overpay. It is a simple cost benefit analysis. Risk versus reward. Is it easy to swallow at
times? No. Is it good business? Yes. I have seen more companies lose their top sales person because they refuse to do
this. This is the sales person who usually brings in 50% of
the company's total sales. Then, the President or Owner
goes crazy when they see the W-2 of the person and finds
out they make more than the President himself. So they
change the compensation plan to satisfy their ego and lose
their best sales person to a competitor who WILL pay that
sales person what they are worth. In the end this costs
the organization far more in lost sales and profits. There
are certain people you can't afford to lose—overpay those
people.

If you want to really develop a high performance organization and retain people in the process, your compensation plan needs to support attracting and retaining the
BEST people. The best pay model for your business is one
that Tom Peters points out in "Good to Great." Worthing-
ton Steel uses it. Hire five people, work them like ten and
pay them like eight. Take a guess what type of people you
attract. People who want to **bust their butts!** You get top
performers because they can make more with your company than at other places but are willing to put out to get
it. It's not what you pay them, it's what you get for what
you pay them. This model is a magnet for high performers.
You will also see that poor performers will be driven out of
an organization like this by their co-workers or self-select
out, because they don't want to work that hard. Either
way, you win as an organization. This is **the** best way to
handle compensation from a retention and performance

perspective. It is a great way to eliminate the money factor from the retention equation. It is also at the heart of building a high-performing organization. More importantly, you have just put money on your bottom line if you are a CEO, GM or owner. High performers pay for themselves.

Benefits

Studies have also shown that employees who are satisfied with their benefits are far more likely to stay. No surprise there—most people do realize the value of their benefits and mentally factor it into what they view as compensation for the work they do. Most people *do not* realize how much is in their total compensation and that needs to be communicated to them. They also need to realize the impact on the bottom line to the organization. In many cases, they don't care. Most people though, even the most stubborn people, will grudgingly admit that a company has to make a profit so that they can have a job.

When I worked in Human Resources, I always told employees to talk to their neighbor about what the neighbor gets as benefits and then to come back in because I was curious to know what other companies were doing. Why would I encourage this? Because in the vast majority of cases I was pretty sure that our benefits were better. Hey, I already had my surveys and **knew** where we stood in the marketplace. I just forced the employee to do their own "market survey."

Picking the right benefits is imperative so you are not spending your money in the wrong places. First, analyze your workforce and find out what is valued. Listen to what they are saying. People will talk. When they do, ask the probing questions to understand what is important to them. Then, design your benefits structure around those needs so you are not wasting money to begin with. Each work force is different. You need to be flexible and creative. Don't use a one-size-fits-all approach. I tell people that not everyone likes the same TV dinner. Personally, I like the Banquet TV dinner for $1 that has salisbury steak, corn and mashed potatoes. I am not a fan of the turkey meal with the turkey, mashed potatoes, and peas. If served the turkey dinner, I will only eat the turkey and the mashed potatoes and throw the rest away. Benefits are the same way. Offer options on the various benefits so people can pick what they like. If you are doing that, you have taken a step to eliminate the attraction of another company's benefit plan as a factor in whether or not to leave. Employees are far more savvy today and seriously take benefits into consideration as they are looking at the opportunity. An organization can spend a bundle of money on a high end benefit plan, some of which certain employees may not even value. If you offer them the flexibility to pick and chose, you can offer more than the average, without breaking the bank because you are not wasting money on benefits that they don't care about. In fact, offering flexibility in benefits are generally less expensive than a one-size-fits-all benefit plan (Choquette, 2016)

Almost as important as the benefits you offer, is the ease of access to those benefits. Ease of access and a hassle-free usage is key. I have seen organizations with incredibly generous plans that people hated because they were difficult to access or when problems arose, nobody was there to help them solve the problem. Don't confuse "self-service" benefits with excellent service. In most cases we have moved to self-service and it could more aptly be described as "no service." The result is employees who are not happy with their benefit plan, do not see it as valuable and therefore it is not a positive factor in retention. If that's the case, you have just spent a huge amount of money and gotten no retention benefit from a major cost item.

The answer to the dilemma is a solid benefit plan that is easy for your people to access and where help is available if they have a problem! It doesn't get any simpler than that!

> Pull out your most recent pay and benefits survey and spot check what you are paying several of your solid people to see how you compare. If you sense some issues, trust your gut and look to see if your pay and benefits are competitive. If not, take a look at the rest of your pay structure. (Note: If you don't have a pay and benefits survey, get one and start the process!)

> Look to see the differential in pay between your best performers and your average performers. Is it greater than 10%? If not, develop a plan to quickly to address it.

On a final note about pay and benefits, i.e. total compensation, (Not rewards!) Is the total compensation issue an easy one? Absolutely not. You need a well-thought-out strategy that gives employees what they need. This will enable you to retain your best people and still allow you to remain profitable. It is not as difficult as you may believe, and if done properly can effectively remove "money" as a negative factor and, in many cases, give you an advantage over your competition.

Flexibility

When deciding where to put this section I debated between after the "Benefits" section and after the "Caring" section because flexibility is a recognition that our lives are hectic and that you as a leader understand that. It also shows that by being flexible you care enough to work with your people to make their lives easier. Most people view flexibility as a **huge benefit!** Your flexibility can be ad hoc or formal within the organization. A Hewitt study indicated that 64% of the surveyed companies indicated it improved retention yet only 27% have company-wide, formal written plans (Sladek, 2008). This topic came up in a round table of the Talent Acquisition Committee in the Metro Milwaukee Society for Human Resource Management chapter which I belong to. Flexibility was cited as the number one area to drive retention in an organization, when faced with limited or reduced budgets/benefits, by this group. It is also a perk that cuts across generations, ethnic groups and gender. In 25 years in human resources, I have **never** heard anyone complain about having additional flexibility in their schedule.

Managers tend to be the biggest determinant of whether or not flexibility is allowed. Unfortunately, managers tend to be paranoid about having to be equal or are worried about abuse so they avoid flexibility. Big mistake! In today's age of limited budgets, flexibility has one huge advantage over other benefits—it's **free.** If you don't give it a try, how will you know if you are throwing out a no-cost retention tool? And, the reality is that most organizations do not put severe restrictions on your ability to be flexible in your department. Why? What do most organizations care about? **Results.** If you are getting the results senior management needs, they are not going to place severe restrictions on you. The question should be not whether or not you should allow flexibility but instead, "If I allow flexibility, will it enable me to get better results while helping me to retain my best people?" If you are getting better results, do you really think the president is going to chew you out because you let someone leave early to go to the doctor?

If you are in Human Resources, you need to be pointing out that people see this as a major benefit and that results are what matter to senior management. As an HR person, you need to make sure you don't get paranoid and tie the hands of your department managers. Allow them to use this powerful tool! Monitor it to ensure abuse is not occurring; or better yet, help your managers to find ways that will enable them to use the tool effectively.

Let's quickly address the issue of the complainer who says, "You aren't being fair!" My question to the complainer is whether or not they are getting their job done. Chances are they aren't! If they aren't, that's probably one of the reasons you don't give them the flexibility you give to the better person. I used to handle this in a simple way when I was in HR. I would tell them the truth. They aren't getting the flexibility because they aren't getting the job done. This discussion may wake them up. By having the discussion, you have also taken another major step in retention by starting to deal with their lousy performance. If they don't like it and quit, you now have an opportunity to hire someone who will perform up to expectations.

Flexibility can take many different forms such as:

- Ability to leave early or come in late to deal with personal issues.

- Summer hours.

- Compressed work week such as 4-day/10-hour shifts. My experience is that once people go to this schedule you will have a war on your hands if you try to go back to the standard 5-day/8-hour shift.

- Allowing employees to work from home all of the time or on certain days.
- Taking vacation in less than half-day increments.
- Part-time work.
- Telecommuting.

This is a short list, a very short list. Flexibility is only limited by your imagination and your desire to try it!

> Sit down with one or two of your fellow managers and discuss areas where you are currently allowing your people flexibility and discuss new areas where you could allow additional flexibility. Then, have each manager try a new one!

TIP

Goal Alignment and a Greater Good

Goal alignment is an intangible element that many organizations forget about. If your employee's goals are in alignment with the company's goals, employees are far more likely to stay because, if they leave, they are abandoning their mission. By doing so, they have made a conscious decision to abandon something that they have believed in for years. The likelihood they will abandon a "belief" is far less than if they are just quitting a *job* at a company.

The best examples of goal alignment in retention are to look at the United States military and non-profit organizations. People don't stay because of the money. They stay because they believe in the mission of the organization and that they are working for something more than money. Their personal goals are intertwined with the mission of the organization. Clearly, no one in the military does it simply for the money.

Another great example of goal alignment and the greater good is the Toro company. Under CEO Ken Melrose, he remade the company as an "environmental" company. The people weren't just making lawn mowers, they were making products that were environmentally friendly. I knew the HR Manager at their large lawn mower plant in Tomah, WI and he would have done anything for the company. That attitude pervaded the workforce because they felt they were contributing to the "greater good" by making environmentally responsible products. Turnover was minimal even before "going green" was vogue.

Can every organization find a mission that people can latch onto that is for the greater good? I believe they can, at least to some extent. Get creative and ask yourself, <u>what does your organization do that makes a difference?</u> When doing recruiting for clients, I take pride in matching people with companies and making a difference in people's lives by propelling their careers forward, not just finding a body to fill an open job requisition for a client company. That goal alignment makes it a lot easier to get up in the morning and to work into the evenings interviewing potential candidates. It was one factor that kept me from

TIP

Develop a list of ways that your organization makes a difference in people's lives or adds to the greater good. Then identify a strategy to convey this to your people. (Ideally, you will do this with several of your managers.)

bailing on my own business during the first three years when times were tight. People in larger organizations are no different.

NO NONSENSE **NOTES**

- Money isn't the main reason people quit.

- Studies show that money is more important to those people earning less than $42,000 per year.

- Hire five people, work them like ten, pay them like eight. You will make money in the process.

- Pay your people fairly. That means top performers get paid more than the average performers!

- One size doesn't fit all when it comes to benefits. Offer your people choices when at all possible.

- Flexibility of schedule is one of the most valued benefits that you can offer people.

SECRET #5: EXPECT PERFORMANCE—DEAL WITH YOUR SLUGS

THIS IS THE one area where managers and organizations tend to fail. They don't manage performance regularly or tell people what they expect from them. If they do tell them what they expect, they often fail to hold them accountable when they don't do what's expected. Instead, they tolerate substandard performance until frustration hits the breaking point and then just bring a person in their office and fire them.

There is nothing that irritates good people more than having to carry the non-performers. Want to take a huge step forward in retention? **Deal with your slugs.** That's it. Real simple. The people who work with them will love you as a boss and, more importantly, respect you! Unfortunately, organizations have become paranoid about firing people. Don't get me wrong, when you fire someone it should be with good reason. It should be properly investigated, documented and ultimately, the termination should be done with the utmost dignity and respect. Nonetheless, you need to deal with your slugs, not only from a business perspective, but from a retention perspective.

The process is simple. Here it is:

- Tell your people what you expect from them.

- Give them the tools and support to get the job done.

- If they don't meet your expectations, bring them in and talk to them. Ask them why and help them problem solve to get them on track.

- If they don't get on track, terminate them, with dignity and respect!

Terminating someone is never easy. When it becomes easy it's time to get out of management because you have probably become callous and uncaring.

NO NONSENSE **NOTES**

- Tell people what you expect from them and hold them accountable for their performance.

- Fire your slugs. Your good performers will love you!

- Terminations should be handled with dignity and respect—always!

SECRET #6:
COMMUNICATE
OR EVAPORATE

A SYSTEMATIC, WELL-STRUCTURED communication process should be at the heart of any employee retention effort. People need to know what is going on, not only from an employee retention perspective, but from an operational perspective. People can't perform at optimal levels if they don't know what is going on. The goal from an employee retention strategy perspective should be to shut down the grapevine and provide information people need to do their jobs, help them feel good about working for your organization, and to feel safe in the organization. The grapevine never produces positive news and it drives negativity and fear, which can be deadly to employee retention.

Negativity and fear are the two emotions that will suck the life out of your organization. It's one thing to not have fun at work.

It's another to have negativity. Negativity can be driven by things such as:

- Pessimistic leadership.
- Tolerating negative behavior or, worse yet, rewarding it
- Lack of appreciation.
- No control over your job.
- Lack of challenge.
- No one listening to you.
- Slow, inaccurate, or incomplete information.
- Excessive workload.

The one thing that should jump out at you is that the manager can impact every one of these items to some extent. The one area that a manager might struggle to deal with is the issue of excessive workload, but the rest of the above list can be successfully influenced by the manager of an area. When I hear the mantra, "I have no control over that," I want to scream. I used to hear those excuses all the time. Stop making excuses and start having an impact.

It starts with you as a manager. You set the tone for your "sphere of influence." If you complain and moan when a directive comes from higher up in the organization, you need to stop doing so immediately. It is demoralizing to your people even if they seem to agree. They know you shouldn't be doing, it so it diminishes you as a leader in their eyes. Worse yet, it sends the message that negativity is acceptable.

When negativity becomes a part of a culture it will be reflected in how people communicate to customers, the quality that is produced and the atmosphere in an organization. When you tour a negative organization you can "smell the stench" of decaying morale. You can feel it in the atmosphere. No one wants to come to work, much less take care of the customer.

If you have negative people in your organization, you need to deal with those people. Sit down with those people and explain what type of behavior you expect and why. When you see them displaying that negativity you need to call them on it and tell them the positive behavior you expect. If you are in a leadership position and you see a member of the management team who works for you engaged in negative behaviors, address it **immediately.** Negative people will sour even the best new hire. It seems that the negative people have to find someone to associate with, probably because nobody else will associate with them. What do these negative people do when you hire a new person? They immediately attach themselves to the new hire and poison their thought process by telling them how evil the organization is, how lousy it is to work there, that the management team are jerks and on and on. They indoctrinate people about how bad the place is.

> Before you say anything negative about something, say two positive things about the situation. This will immediately begin to shift your thought process, and ultimately your behavior, to a positive leadership approach.

Lead by example. Don't add to it by ignoring negative behavior or engaging in it. It's like seeing a fire and letting it burn, or, in some cases, like throwing gas on the fire. Unconsciously, you may find yourself agreeing or joining in. First and foremost, you have to make sure you aren't falling into that trap. You may not like having to do something but you need to keep that to yourself; bite your tongue. If you don't, you undermine the entire leadership structure. Unfortunately, society keeps telling people that management is all screwed up and doesn't care. Your people are bombarded with movies like *Office Space*, *The Devil Wears Prada*, and comic strips like *Dilbert* that depict management in a negative light. You have to counteract that impression as a member of the management team because negativity will make your organization a less desirable place to work, and negatively will impact your ability to retain people.

I have seen organizations purge themselves of negative behavior. It wasn't easy, but they realized that it was necessary. At one organization where I worked, union and management got together and developed a list of 10 positive behaviors that were expected of everyone regardless of level in the organization or whether they were in the union or in management. It wasn't about union or management; it was about your behavior. The development of this list sent a strong message that negative behavior was not acceptable. It worked.

People began to hold each other accountable for not adhering to the 10 positive behaviors. Management was held to a higher standard. The president expected the management team to lead by example.

Check out their list. There is nothing earth-shattering about it. They did it as a company. You can do it as the head of your department, team, facility, or division. You can do it in your "sphere of influence."

10 POSITIVE BEHAVIORS

1. **Show respect** by being courteous and tactful towards others.

2. **Be responsible** by keeping your commitments and being on time.

3. **Enthusiastically cooperate** with others by following procedures, being willing to learn, knowing your job, being receptive and approachable, being open-minded and becoming a team player.

4. **Communicate well** by using appropriate language, praising others and being a good listener.

5. Do your best to **be friendly** and exhibit a good sense of humor.

6. **Be supportive** in the success of others and show concern and caring to your fellow employees.

7. **Use your time well**; be neat, clean and organized.

8. **Be honest** and truthful with yourself and others.

9. Work to your **greatest potential**.

10. **Be fair** in everything you do.

Develop your own list of positive behaviors with your team, department, or facility. Then, put them in writing for everyone to see and start holding each other accountable for following the behaviors. Trust me, you will change quickly after your people call you out on not following the behaviors because they expect you to lead by example. A positive snowball develops fast!

One final word on negativity. After you have stopped the cycle of negativity, and *you can stop the cycle*, you need to start rewarding the people that exhibit the positive behaviors. *When you do that, you will get the spiral moving upward instead of downward!*

Fear

Fear results primarily from three sources:

1. **Uncertainty about the organization's direction and the potential impact on a person's position.**

2. **Punishing people for making mistakes when they take initiative.**

3. **A boss or other senior leadership person who uses fear as a tool to run their area of influence.**

In all cases, the result tends to be the creation of an aversion to risk-taking. Everyone is afraid to say or do what they need to, in order to do the best job possible. They play it safe. Then one day, everyone wakes up to find they can't keep good people or the business has fallen into mediocrity and it is in a death spiral.

Uncertainty about the organization's direction is the easiest to deal with. The answer: communicate with your people. Now wasn't that easy? A well-thought-out communication strategy is **the** best way to effectively drive communication. Don't do it in a haphazard way. Sit down, strategize and develop a well-layered approach using multiple types of communication. By doing so, you make sure everyone hears the message multiple times, and in different media. Use the following list and you will cover 95% of what needs to be covered without having some big fancy system that looks great but wastes time and probably doesn't get through to employees anyway.

- Managers and leaders, at all levels, need to get out in the cubes, factory or on the plant floor and start talking with people daily.
- Have an open door so people come in and ask questions.
- Hold departmental meetings that provide a consistent message, a forum for ideas and a place to bring up concerns about the functioning of the department.
- Hold company, plant, or division meetings that focus on what is going on in the business, plans for the future and how well the business is doing.
- Develop regular postings and updates using email, company intranet or written notices.

A quick note on meetings. Everyone thinks that when I mention meetings that it is some long drawn-out event. Only if you let them be long and drawn out! They can range from five minutes to an hour, depending on what you want to accomplish. In my experience, 90% of the meetings that last an hour or more are just people rambling on. Keep them short, sweet and to the point. The goal of every meeting should be educating people and generating actions that drive results! Information and education will eliminate fear, and drive understanding of what it takes the business to succeed. Both of which reduce turnover and improve how

> If you are not holding regular meetings that 1. educate and 2. generate results, start! Then ask yourself at the end of each meeting if you have accomplished those two objectives.

the business operates as well. Retention does not exist in a vacuum it helps to drive organizational success!

This is the meat and potatoes. Anything beyond these two points is pure gravy. When you get information out and educate your people you will virtually shut down the negative influence of the internal grapevine. By doing so, you eliminate speculation, uncertainty, and self-serving communication. When you do that, you have just significantly reduced several major sources of fear. The beautiful thing about this approach, even if you are only a supervisor or manager, you can do most of these things in your "sphere of influence." So even if the organization chooses not to do some of these things, you can still make an impact!

In recent years, experts have begun using the term "bullying" to describe what I would term "fear." It is an abusive pattern of behavior that creates uncertainty and a nagging sense of fear in an employee's mind. Call it fear or bullying, the effect is the same. It kills optimal performance and drives turnover. It's that simple.

Fear is something that rarely pervades the entire organization. More often than not, it is found in pockets of the organization where a toxic boss has been allowed to act with impunity or is politically astute and hides their tactics of leading by fear. Unless the organization deals with this manager, the organization risks sending a damaging message to *all* employees that it is willing to condone inappropriate managerial behavior. The people in other departments will then wonder if this could happen to them while the organization looks the other way.

By not dealing with an abusive boss, the organization looks clueless, or worse yet, seems to condone this behavior. This can be a key decision point for a person when looking at whether or not to leave because it plants the seed in an employee's mind that the organization simply does not care about people in general. Mentally, a person will use this as a way to rationalize moving even if they work for a good boss. It makes it easier to turn in that resignation when offered another job.

The unfortunate thing about fear is that sometimes it comes from a key person in the organization such as the head of a division, plant manager, or a vice president who is successful in their own right. These people hide behind mantras like, "I expect the best from my people and that's why they don't like me," or "They quit because they couldn't stand the pressure," or the best of all, "I provided them with a great training ground so now they are able to take that next step in their career." When people see a senior-level person getting away with ruling by fear, they will have an inherent distrust of the organization. They will not openly express their thoughts, but they will when talking with their co-workers, when out to lunch, or having a drink after work. There will be a very low buzz in the organization. If you are looking for open comments to verify high-level fear before addressing a problematic senior-level person, you will never address the problem because people aren't dumb enough to commit political suicide openly.

How do you know you have a problem?

- **You will see your best managers who work under this person leaving; they don't have to put up with this and won't!**

- **You will get guarded and very carefully worded responses to questions about what is going on in that division or area.**

- **You hear the buzz regularly that someone is a "jerk." I am being kind because the words they will use are often sandwiched between a few expletives.**

- People will make slight innuendos when they talk about how the department is run.
- Employees start to request transfers to other areas of the organization.
- A good employee leaves and that person will be "too busy" to fill out the exit interview form.
- On a rare occasion, you may have a good employee leave, transfer or outright quit without another job, and they will walk into your office, unload on you, and tell you that they are telling you this with the understanding that it is "off the record" and do not want it being shared because they do not want to burn any bridges.

Ask yourself if any of the above points occur in your organization. If they do, start asking questions about those items because chances are, you have a problem.

In most cases, the only way you will know there is a problem is that you will get bits and pieces of all of the above. A great big jigsaw puzzle begins to form that is always missing a few pieces to create a finished picture. At that point, you have a tough decision (that's why they pay you the big bucks!). You can look the other way or you can, instead, take some action to address the issue decisively.

If you are in tune with your people, you will have seen the signs all along so the puzzle will have been taking shape over time. Ideally, you will have been bringing these issues forward to the people that need to know about them. Hopefully, they will have stepped in, communicated decisively with the problematic manager and the manager will have changed their behavior. If they are unwilling or unable, I suggest you start questioning whether or not it is the type of organization **you** want to work in!

As a department manager, you may have to deal with a boss who uses bullying or fear as a way to manage. Your job, whether you like it or not, is to insulate your people from your boss. If you don't, you will bear the brunt of dealing with the aftermath of the turnover your boss generates.

NO NONSENSE **NOTES**

- You set the tone in your "sphere of influence."

- Deal with your negative people. Change them or remove them!

- Tell your people the behaviors you expect from *every one of them*.

- Communicate in multiple ways and at multiple levels to optimize communication.

- Keep your meetings short!

- Meetings are designed to educate and to drive results.

- Deal with toxic managers. Where there is smoke, there is usually fire.

SECRET #7:
HELP THEM GROW
OR WATCH THEM GO!

Orientation and Assimilation

Orientation and assimilation are the first steps in growing a person within the organization. How you assimilate people sets the stage for their future growth. The goals of an orientation are simple:

- Assimilate the person into the organization.
- Make them productive as quickly as possible.
- Educate them about the organizational culture and values.
- Complete the necessary paperwork to comply with the law, get people paid and enroll them in benefits programs.

When it comes to retention, the first three are the most important. Unfortunately, most organizations have orientations that appear to be targeted to completing the last item. Orientation is not all about completing the paperwork!

A major reason for having a systematic, gradual and well thought out orientation is to assimilate the person into the organization. Your goal is to integrate the new employee into the culture, its values and goals of the organization, and to establish expectations. This is the time that the organization truly has the employee's ear. They are listening and want to hear what the organization is all about. If you don't fill that void, who will? Answer: the worst employee in the place who complains and moans about everything. They attach themselves to a new employee like a leech in a swamp and begin sucking the life out of the new employee. If you don't fill the communication void, someone will (and it's usually some loser!)

Here is the typical first day in most places. Several hours with the HR administrator filling out paperwork and being given the handbook to sign. Forget reading the thing much less understanding the key points, just sign it so we have something for the file! If the newbie is lucky, they will have an office ready and be set up with a computer, email account, phone system and at least a stapler and some office supplies. In this day and age of high tech software, systems and advanced manufacturing techniques, this is an absolute must to bring a person up to speed so that they can become a productive member of the organization. It's bad enough going to a new organization where you don't know anyone much less not have the basic tools needed to get the job done.

The new employee shakes their head and wonders what type of organization they have joined when a lousy orientation takes place. You can hear this sucking sound as all the positive energy, excitement, and enthusiasm about the new job that existed prior to starting is drained from that employee. A lousy orientation is incredibly moronic from a productivity perspective, but also from a retention standpoint.

You expend all of the time and effort to attract and land top talent but then just throw them in and let them learn as they go. There is no organized plan, or there's one that, on its surface, appears organized but fails to take into account that a person can only absorb so much in one day. It is the classic example of putting 10 pounds of poop in a 5-pound bag! *People can't sit through eight hours of orientation!*

People are nervous, scared and uncertain for the first few days on the job. Their anxiety level is at an all time high. They are extremely vulnerable to counter offers from their former employers. Face it, counter offers are a major problem when bringing a new employee on board. Often organizations counter offer after an employee gives notice. They also listen to see if an employee is vulnerable to a counter shortly after the move. Smart employers purposely stay in touch with former employees to listen for the signs of discontent and then capitalize on that discontent with an overture to that employee who may be having second thoughts about the move. I know I did as an HR director. I purposely had their friends from our company contact them to see how they were doing. If we sensed there might be receptivity to returning to our organization, we attacked that vulnerability like a battalion of tanks during the Battle of the Bulge in WWII. We had nothing to lose and everything to gain!

Orientation is not hard, unfortunately we see it as processing paperwork or an annoyance. I have several simple guidelines to make orientations **simple** and **effective**. All you have to do is:

- Have a formal process with the steps documented so you don't miss anything. A simple checklist is all you need.

- Have someone enthusiastic lead the orientation process.

- Break your orientation up over several days or weeks.

- Never go longer than three hours with the person sitting in a room filling out forms or going over policies.

- Include the immediate supervisor in the process because the people don't report to HR. Let the new person get to know their immediate supervisor right from the start.

- Expect the supervisor or manager to have a documented education schedule. The sink or swim method may work, but it also results in the drowning of a lot of good employees!

- Have senior level people introduce themselves during orientation and, ideally, have them present part of the orientation. This will wow the new employee that someone in senior management actually took the time to play a role in the orientation process.

- Make sure the tools they need to do the job are waiting for them on the first day, including desk, computer, phone and basic supplies.

- Assign a buddy to shadow this person for a period of time, someone who will take the time to be with that person. Pick one of your great employees who believes in the organization, so you build on the positive energy the employee has when they start a new job. This should be someone who can show them how things really get done and where to go for resources.

Remember, if you don't select that person, the biggest complainer will find the employee and do your orientation for you!

- Develop a list of FAQs for the new person, along with names of people to contact with key questions.

- Introduce them to people. That is simple courtesy. When guests show up at a party do you greet them and say "See ya later?" You don't; you want them to feel welcome. A new employee is no different.

- Never have the employee eat lunch alone for the first several weeks. It is critical that they become socialized into the organization and feel a part of their new home. Don't underestimate the power that social relationships have in workplace retention. In one organization I worked for we noticed that if a person was not eating lunch with someone at the end of the first week, retention dropped significantly. That's when we started the buddy system and assigned someone to hang with this person to make them feel at home, and it worked. We also knew then, if the newbie had concerns so that we could address them.

- Set regular intervals to check in with the new person to see how they are doing. If you listen to the person's responses, you will pick up on signals that the new person is struggling, then act on the signals.

The elements above work! Just look at any branch of the US military. The military does the best job of any organization in the training and assimilating of diverse populations into one cohesive group that will work together towards a common goal that I have ever seen. If you have veterans in your organization, tap into their expertise and they can tell you how the best do it! Use the elements above as a starting point, add your vet's expertise and build a dynamite orientation that will enhance your retention.

> **TIP**
>
> Get a group of managers together and brainstorm items that will drive retention as well as make new employees more productive in a shorter period of time. Then, start to rebuild your orientation.

When I teach my C.R.A.P. Leadership System©, I tell my students that people are like tomato plants. You should see the odd looks I get, at first. You can plant a garden with tomato plants and do nothing else except leave it up to Mother Nature. Sometimes the plants grow if you are lucky enough to get rain and the weeds don't stunt the growth of the plants. But we all know there is a better way. Water the plants, weed the garden and perhaps even fertilize it. What do you get? A more prolific garden with better tomatoes! Well, people are like tomatoes. If you give them some attention they will grow, and thrive.

How many people actually know what they want in their career? I dare say, not a whole lot! Encourage your people to think about their career, especially your young people. Most young people coming out of school have no clue what they want to do in their career. I know I really didn't, even though I thought I did. In many cases their parents never give them any guidance and, if they do, how many kids do you know will listen to their parents? I have spoken with hundreds of people about their careers. Do you think as the parent of three kids that my kids listen to their dad? Maybe a little, but not nearly as much as they should. As their boss, they are more likely to listen to **you** than anyone else because their paychecks are impacted by you.

Encourage people to think about their careers in the context of their life. Until about ten years ago, I never did. One day I stumbled on Jeff Gitomer's yellow book, "Yes Attitude" simply by accident. It started me on a journey that has led me to read motivational speakers like Jim Rohn, Tony Robbins and dozens of others. Then I actually laid out a game plan. The game plan has led to planning and building for the future and I realized that I had wasted many years of my life because of a lack of a life plan. My career is only one piece of that plan. If you can get your people thinking about their career in the context of their life they will develop a sense of purpose, be more driven, accomplish more, and be far happier with their life and their job. Who reaps the benefits? Certainly they do, but so do you! It enables you to help them perform better and be ready to take that next step in the organization. In my experience, young people often leave jobs too early because they do not feel as if they are growing or are going nowhere. They usually are growing but they just don't know it. It's your job as a manager to point that out to them, or if they aren't going anywhere, get them pointed in the right direction. I recently recruited a high-potential engineer who felt his company had no plans for him. Even though they had alluded to him that he would play a role in future expansion of the organization they had never really talked to him about their thoughts. After he gave his notice, they suddenly started to lay out all the specific ideas they had for him. Too late—his mind was made up and he is now in an organization that has developmental plans for its people.

In many organizations, there is no place for people to be promoted because they are too small or upward advancement is not available but, there is **always** room for people to grow. By keeping people growing, you will retain people far longer than if you neglect them. In a study done by Sibson Consulting it was found that "work content is always the largest motivator of good performance and the most consistent driver of retention, regardless of age." (Sibson, 2006) Eventually, the person who values "growth" may leave anyway, but if they feel they are growing, they are far more likely to stick around a bit longer. Just because the organization does not have a formal plan to help people grow does not mean you as a department manager can't have growth plans for your people. Be the exception! When other department managers lose their sharp talent every two years, you will keep yours for three or perhaps four years. You have just doubled the retention of every other department.

Career development is not only for the young. As people progress in their career, they still want to know where they are going. Even if they have no desire to be promoted, most people love to take on new challenges to keep from being bored. When boredom sets in, people get restless and begin to wonder if the grass isn't greener on the other side of the fence. Keeping these people in place and engaged is a way to strengthen your department and avoid the instability created by turnover. Your longer service people can be the people that will sustain you in difficult times.

The easiest way to get the ball rolling on developing your people is to ASK them what they want. Most times, they will not be able to tell you. If they do, that's great. Then you can work with them to make sure their expectations align with your department and company goals. By asking, you have put the ball in their court and they will do most of the work. After all, it's their career. You just have to be there to provide support and assist them in **their** growth. Your job is not to take ownership of their plan. Your job is to get them thinking, planning and monitor if they are acting on their plan. *This does not have to be some big fancy process.* Ask them, discuss ideas, develop ways to help them get there and show them how they can put the plan into action. It's simple. I like it simple.

In his book *Leadership,* Lee Thayer outlines that a leader has an obligation to not let his people default on themselves. By asking and expecting your people to act on what they develop, you prevent them from defaulting on their career and, in many cases, their lives. By expecting them to perform, you help people to optimize their potential.

NO NONSENSE **NOTES**

- If you don't conduct orientation, your worst employee will do it for you.

- Orientation should be more than just filling out paperwork.

- Keep your orientation sessions less than three hours in length. Hold more sessions if need be, but don't go over more than three hours for any session.

- Pair your new employee with a buddy to guide them through the first few months.

- Ask your people what they want.

- People are like tomatoes—they won't grow if they don't get nourishment.

- Growth can occur in your job or within the company.

- Top performers will not tolerate a lack of growth.

- Work content is a consistent driver of retention, regardless of age.

SECRET #8: **VISIBILITY, MANAGEMENT BY WALKING AROUND**

THIS IS THE Holy Grail of retention. It is the Holy Grail of Management. Tom Peters said it 20 years ago in "In Search of Excellence." The executives at Xerox got it when they designed a training program (more than 30 years ago) so managers would get out of their offices. Visibility is timeless. Yet, we tend to return to the caves we call our offices and hibernate. We cut ourselves off from our people and the information we need to run our business. We also cut out one of the most effective retention tools at our disposal—visibility.

Early in my career as an Employee Relations Supervisor (yes, it was about our relationship with our employees back in the day, as my son would say), I worked with a General Manager who took over a facility that was in major trouble. Productivity was terrible, delivery times were abysmal and morale was so low nobody wanted to come to work. When he took over the facility, the first thing he did was begin taking his morning and afternoon stroll through the facility. This was a sprawling operation that ran 24/7 with rotating shifts so it was incredibly hard to communicate with employees, much less see them in person. Not for him. He went out every morning and afternoon like clockwork. 7AM and 3PM. He'd stroll around the facility and chat with the third shift as they were leaving and the first shift as they were starting in the morning. Then he would catch the first shift people going off and the second shift people coming on. People loved talking with him and he knew everyone. He also knew everything that was going on in the operation. He was able to use that information to make operational decisions that drove success. In a matter of months, productivity was up, delivery times were down, accidents were reduced and morale was on the rise. The facility was making money and people were glad to come in every shift. He spent two hours a day being highly visible. In fact, people noticed when he wasn't around! They loved it. They loved him. And, he learned more about what was going on operationally and with our people.

For some odd reason, managers in offices and white-collar environments are far less visible than those in manufacturing areas. Ironically, in most white-collar environments, you are usually dealing with people who all work on a day shift making it easier to access all of your people.

If you take away one thing from this book, this is it. It's simple. Real simple. **Get out of your office.** That's the answer. If you get out of your office, walk around the facility, observe, listen and say "hello" to people, you have moved light years past the vast majority of your competition. Instead of texting someone or sending an email, walk down the hall and talk to them. This may come as a shock to most managers but your people actually *like* seeing you and talking to you. Walking around will make you unique in management today. Why? Because everyone sits in their office or cube and emails the person two feet away, or texts them. With all the electronic communication means at our disposal it gives us excuses to not be visible. Consequently, we have made it easy to hide in the office and avoid face-to-face communication.

The very communication technology that was supposed to make us an "information" based society is cutting us off from our people—people that provide us with information! We find ourselves emailing and texting the people in the cube next to us. That's great if we are dealing with a simplistic issue. Unfortunately, most the issues with people are **not** simplistic. Email and texting is not what's called a "channel rich" communication method because it eliminates the key ingredients in communication: voice tone, facial expression, and body language.

E-mail and texting also fails to give us a chance to know who our people are, what's important to them, what they like about working here, and why they stay. How many people do you know who will tell you in an email their teenage daughter is pregnant or that their wife's cancer treatments are going well? None that I know of. For those of you who are thinking, "That's none of my business," I have one thing to say to you: it is your business. Those are issues that distract people from doing their job and being energized at work. If you can help, it makes you human and people like to work for someone who cares. Why? Because too many bosses don't. If people don't want to talk about it, that's perfectly fine too. But if they do you just blew a great opportunity to get to know your people and what makes them tick, or if the watch is broken! My experience is that most people love to talk to other people about what's going on in their lives. When you talk with your people face-to-face, you have given yourself a leg up on your competition in the retention war.

Unfortunately, the bulk of our message is conveyed by body language and non-verbal means that we lose so much in the translation when we communicate on the phone, via email, texting and even written memo. This leads to mis-communication, confusion and a host of other problems. Only 7% of your message is conveyed in words. 38% is sent via body language and the remaining 55% is sent in non-verbal ways such as facial expressions and voice tone. No wonder people take that email or text the wrong way when they get it! (Certo, 2009)

The result of hiding behind electronics is that we now have a generation of managers who do not know how to walk around, make small talk, and in many cases are afraid to talk to people in person.

The President and owner at one of my clients, walks through the office and the shop four times a day. He always makes it a point to walk around before he leaves so he sees everyone on the second shift. This provides people an opportunity to ask questions, bring up issues/concerns, find out how business is going, etc. It gives him an opportunity to take the pulse of the organization, examine product quality, and communicate with the people. Here's how it works.

- **Visibility drives accessibility.**
- **Accessibility creates an opportunity to communicate.**
- **Communication drives an opportunity to solve problems.**
- **Problem solving builds credibility and it also helps your productivity and quality.**

- Credibility builds trust.
- People like people they can trust.
- If they like you, they are far less likely to leave!
- Therefore, visibility drives retention!

The other operational benefits are enormous as well. You will spot quality problems, workflow issues, or customer service needs as you walk around. Walking around will make you money, while driving retention in the process.

The best way to ensure that you are visible is to develop a regular routine for walking around. Put it on your calendar like any other meeting. After all, you are going out to meet with people. Twice a day is the minimum. Take a walk around first thing in the morning and late in the day at a minimum. First thing in the morning gives you an opportunity to see if there are issues that need to be addressed, if your people need anything, or to pass along critical information. Late in the day enables you to see if there are issues so you can adjust for tomorrow or information you need to convey that they will need for the next day. It also gives you an opportunity to chat with your people in person, not online.

These strolls give you an opportunity to interact, to get to know your people. They create opportunities to communicate. People become comfortable talking with you. As you communicate you soon learn what is important to people. That is critical as you have performance management discussions and career growth sessions. You will learn what these people are jazzed about doing. That insight is invaluable. Besides, you will actually have fun doing it! If you don't, you need to get out of management!!!!!

You will also get an opportunity to know your people as people. This insight is crucial because it will enable you to notice changes in their behavior. Changes that indicate that something may be wrong at work. Changes that may indicate that they are thinking of leaving! If you sense those things, a red flag should go up something is wrong and you need to ask questions to determine what it is. Then take action!

Behavior changes can also be indicative of issues people are facing outside of work. Those issues impact a person's ability to perform on the job. 20% of the people at work, at any one time, are facing issues that distract from their focus on their job. The cost to your business is staggering.

Worse yet, behavior changes may also be signals that someone is at the tipping point. Forklift accidents used to be the number one cause of fatalities in the workplace. Today, the number one cause of fatalities is violence. Your visibility just may enable you to observe behaviors and to pick up on issues that are red flags of potential violent behavior. You can then take steps to head it off by working with your Human Resources department to intervene with professional resources.

When giving my "Give Your Employees C.R.A.P...and 7 Other Secrets to Employee Retention" speech, I am shocked to hear from my audiences that less than 5% of

> Block out 30-60 minutes twice a day on your calendar indicating that you are in an "employee meeting," and instead get out of your office and stroll around the cubes or factory floor. You're not lying, you will be meeting with all of your people—just not in a conference room. Schedule it and stroll around!

the participants get out of their offices and stroll around daily. These are a mix of department managers, human resources managers and senior level executives. What's their excuse? I don't have the time. My response? It's your job—make the time. You are there to lead people. The best way to lead them is to talk to them, and visibility is the best way to create opportunities to talk to them.

Getting out and strolling around is the best way to make yourself accessible. And, you are far easier to approach when you walk right by someone in the aisle. It makes it easy for people to stop you and ask you questions. Questions they might not ask if they had to get up, walk into your office and disturb you. That's why the stroll is the best way to create accessibility, but it is not the only way.

You can also be accessible when you are in your office. I grew up in the old school when we talked about an "open door policy." Literally, it was an open door. If you had your door closed, you could expect the General Manager to ask you why. The answer better be a good one! Keeping your door open sends a powerful message that you are accessible to your people. If they walk by and see the door open, they will be more likely to stop in and talk to you about something that is going on.

Your back should never be to the door. You might as well put up a sign that says, "Don't bother me." I worked in one organization where the General Manager sat with her back to the door and she worked on her computer all the time. She was the object of numerous jokes because of it. And no one ever stopped in to talk to her. No one! She had no credibility and no one trusted her. It also set the tone for the other managers in the organization that it was perfectly fine to not be accessible.

Part of the accessibility is the "vibe" you send off about whether or not you are accessible. Even if your door is

Keep your door open at least 80% of the time, unless you are engaged in a confidential meeting or call.

open, often you are on the phone or engaged in some activity and an employee stops by and sees you busy. Don't let them leave; signal them to wait. Motion them to sit down. I used to give them the two-minute warning sign so they knew it would be quick. Then, if at all possible, cut the call off ASAP. These are your people we are talking about and they drive your success. They wouldn't be coming by unless they valued your opinion, needed you, or needed something. The message you send is powerful. They are more important than some person on the phone. If you make them wait, tell them who it was on the phone. Why? It's important to let them know why you kept them waiting. You wouldn't keep your boss waiting. Frankly, your people may be more important than your boss. There were times when I would tell my boss I would call her back because an employee was waiting to see me. That is powerful. You have just sent the message that your employee is more important than the boss. It makes the employee feel good about you and themselves. Your people drive your success and the success of your department, plant, office, etc. Success keeps the boss happy. Get it?

When you make the employee wait or tell them to come by later, guess what happens? They stop coming by your office. It's like being rejected on a date; it doesn't take long before you stop asking after being rejected. More importantly, most people rarely stop by just to spend time chatting. They need guidance, want your thoughts, or need something in order to get their job done. Your lack of availability has probably hurt their productivity and created frustration with that employee.

Being available for your people is like being available for your kids. When your kids need you, they need or want you at that moment, not 15 minutes from now. They are ready to talk. Talk to them because, if you don't, chances are when you do get back to them 15, 20, or maybe 45 minutes later, they have figured it out or don't want to talk anymore. The response you will get is something like this, "No big deal, it wasn't anything important." Do you really believe that? If you do you're kidding yourself. It was important and you blew an opportunity to communicate because you weren't available. I hear people talk about quality time with your kids. That's a feel-good phrase to cover for the lack of time we spend with our kids. I once heard it said when my kids were young that *anytime with your kids is quality time!* Your people are no different.

NO NONSENSE **NOTES**

- Get out of your office, take a stroll, and get face-to-face with your people every day!

- Visibility drives retention.

- Find out what makes your people tick.

- 93% of your message comes from body language, your voice tone, and other non-verbal ways.

- At any given time, 20% of your workforce has personal issues that may affect their work performance.

- Maintain a real open door policy.

- Any time with your people is quality time.

- Never sit with your back to the door; it sends the message you are not accessible.

- Make time for your people; avoid telling someone to "come back later" when they come to your office.

- Your door should be open 80% of the time, send the message that you are available and accessible to your people.

CONCLUSION:

WHAT'S MY NUMBER, AND HOW DO I MAKE IT BETTER?

BY NOW YOU should know what your turnover is. If you have been doing the "Tips" you have already started to put together a comprehensive strategy to increase your retention. Now, consciously sit down with several of your fellow managers, or your staff if you are a senior executive, and brainstorm other ideas based on the various sections of the book. This is where everyone starts to get nervous. You actually have to get off your duff and do something. That's why I wrote this book in the format I did. Hopefully, you will have been trying the "Tips" all along and my request isn't like taking a leap off of a cliff without a safety harness. But, if you are feeling some nervousness, here is a story that may help you.

As an HR Director in a software development firm where turnover was a constant problem because of the nature of the business and other issues we were experiencing, here's how I built our retention strategy. I sat down with managers, VPs, my boss, software developers-anyone who would sit down with me. We came up with ideas. I had this huge whiteboard that was 4 feet high by 15 feet long in my office. We put the ideas on the board. Everyone in the company could see them when they walked by my office, people stopped in and added to them and then we started doing what we had on the board. Guess what? It worked. Not only did the ideas improve retention, we actually saw an improvement in other business metrics like customer service, productivity, and quality as well. My boss, the president, saw the results, and so did the managers who helped me with it. The corporation got what they wanted—higher profits—and we had a better place to work. That's the bottom line. And I started from scratch! You are half way there if you have been doing the "Tips." Just keep adding to them and your retention strategy will be formed.

Are you ready to take that leap? Will you live happily ever after? If you take that leap, the result will be both personally and professionally rewarding. I leave you with this quote as a final thought to give you the courage to move forward.

*Far better is it to dare mighty things, to win
glorious triumphs, even though checkered by failure,
than to rank with those poor spirits who neither enjoy
nor suffer much, because they live in a gray twilight
that knows not victory nor defeat.*

Teddy Roosevelt

BIBLIOGRAPHY

Buckingham, Marcus, and Coffman, Curt. *First, Break All the Rules.* Simon & Schuster, New York, NY 1999.

Certo, S.C. *Modern Management: Diversity, Quality, Ethics and the Global Environment.* 11th ed., Allyn and Bacon, Upper Saddle River, NJ, 2009.

Choquette, Francois. "Benefits: One Size No Longer Fits All." *Insurance Thought Leadership*, 8 Aug. 2016. www.insurancethoughtleadership.com/benefits-one-size-no-longer-fits-all.

Christensen, John, Lundin, Stephen, and Paul, Harry. *Fish Tales.* ChartHouse Learning, New York, NY, 2002.

Collins, Jim. *Good to Great.* HarperBusiness, New York, NY, 2001.

Gitomer, Jeffrey. *Little Gold Book of YES! Attitude.* FT Press, Upper Saddle River, NJ, 2007.

Sanborn, Mark. *The Fred Factor.* Doubleday, New York, NY, 2004.

"Title of this Study." Sibson Consulting, 12 Oct. 2016, www.sibson.com/publications/surveysandstudies/2006/Rowno5.pdf. Accessed 12 Oct. 2016.

Slodek, Carol. "Hewitt Survey Suggests U.S. Companies Not Effectively Managing Workplace Flexibility Programs." *Business Wire*, 30 Apr. 2008, Businesswire.com/news/home/20080430005229/en/Hewitt-suggests-US-cmpanies-effectively-managing. Accessed 12 Oct. 2016.

Thayer, Lee. *Leadership: Thinking, Being, Doing.* WME Books, Rochester, NY, 2007.

CREATING A
CULTURE OF C.R.A.P.®

If you are interested in employee retention, leadership or making millennials great keynotes or workshops based on the principles of C.R.A.P., contact Human Asset Management LLC:

Phone: **414-421-9626**
E Mail: **jeff@jeffkortes.com**
Online: **jeffkortes.com**
Address: **Human Asset Management LLC**
           PO Box 320294
           Franklin, WI 53132

Sign up for Jeff's blog: **jeffkortes.com**
Follow Jeff on Twitter: **@JeffKortes**

To purchase bulk copies of *Give Your Employees C.R.A.P.*® at a discount, call 414-421-9626.